The Value Packed Superheroes!

Spreading Values Around The World

Dear Walter Children,

Y'all are amazing. Continue to Spread Values around the world!

—

This book is dedicated to children and
all who help spread positive values around the world.

Copyright © 2021 by Dr. Talaya L. Tolefree

Written by Dr. Talaya L. Tolefree

All rights reserved. No part of this book may be used or reproduced in any manner whatsoever without the prior written permission of the author.

I am Hezekiah and I help spread the value Humanity around the world!

Humanity

"We all must show love and respect for humanity. Together we can be all we can be, showing a sense of morality." Hezekiah explained.

Joy
"I am happy when I play with my friends! I have joy because they show me their love never ends!" Joyanna said.

Best Friends Forever

I am Aiden and I help spread the value Accountability around the world!

Fairness

"Bring awareness to the need for fairness. We need fairness at home, school and community, being fair helps build unity!" Fatima explained.

I am Emily and I help spread the value Empathy around the world!

Empathy

"I know how D'Sean felt when he fell and hurt his knee. I remember how I felt when I fell from my Grandma's Appletree." Emily said as she helped D'Sean.

I am Justina and I help spread the value Justice around the world!

I am Peter and I help spread the value Peace around the world!

HUMANITY
JOY
ACCOUNTABILITY
FAIRNESS
EMPATHY
JUSTICE
PEACE
LOVE

Join us in helping our children learn more about values. As a collective, we can work together to help one another practice living the values on each page. Adults, Parents and Educators, take a Sankofa Moment and reflect on your childhood, do you remember how you were taught about values? Which values do you hold close today? How do you learn about values that are important to others? Which values do we need most in our world today? How do you teach others about values? There are lots of fun and creative ways to use this book to teach the importance of values by engaging in a variety of activities using the values on each page:

Create Your Own Activities to Start Conversations About Values:
- Friendship Activities - What values do you need to be a good friend?
- Transportation Activities – Choose a value to discuss in the car, bus, airplane or on a bike ride.
- Leadership Activities - How can you use values to be a good leader?

Pre-Teach Values as Vocabulary Words:
- Make connections with prior knowledge/experience with values.
- Use visuals to help explain values.
- Create a piece of art that expresses values.
- Create a poem/story about values.

Have a Value Packed Week:
Choose a value of the week, add prompts to start conversations about values:
- Think about why the value is important.
- How can you use the value to fix friendships?
- Have you or a friend ever used the value?
- Think about ways you can practice the value for yourself.
- How can you help others practice the value?
- Challenge children to use their superhero powers to detect when a value has been used or when a value could have been used at home, school or community.

Have fun shaping our next generation of Superhero leaders!

Made in the USA
Middletown, DE
12 July 2022